WE WERE WARRIORS
JOHNNY NO BUENO

No Bueno

AND MC HANK

We Were Warriors

by Johnny No Bueno

This book published by University of Hell Press.
www.universityofhellpress.com

© 2012 Johnny No Bueno

Book Design by Vince Norris
www.norrisportfolio.com

Cover by McHank
www.McHank.com

"Stand Your Ground" and "Gin" first appeared in *Present Tense: Folio Two* by Hubris Press, 2011.

"Maldito" and "Shod Foot" first appeared in *Sparrow Ghost Anthology Volume 2*, 2012.

Dropkick Murphys. "Hang 'Em High." from *Going Out In Style*. (Born & Bred Records. 2011.) Lyrics reprinted with permission of the artist.

Published in the United States of America.
ISBN 978-1-938753-01-5

Table of Contempts

This book is dedicated to America's forgotten youth. It is dedicated to the Portland, San Francisco, New York, and Boston punx, skins, and hardcore kids, my friends from the Seals on 5th and Morrison, to the scumbags from Haight Street, Hollywood, Tompkins Square, and Harvard Square; the highways and railways, the juvenile detentions, county jails, insane asylums, detoxes, the gutters, and housing projects. You will always remain the reason I get up in hopes of exacting the revenge your ghosts scream me awake with every morning.

This book is dedicated to my father, Ian Barton Bowers, Marty Kruse, and all the other dead ones whose bones have paved the way to my redemption: Tomorrow, Damian, Rushin', Poopdick Chris, Vomit, Hatred, Strawberry Jason, Homebum Scotty, Loose Bruce, and Smiley to name a few.

We Were Warriors

We were warriors.
We championed listless causes.
We sat penniless daring autumn to smack us rainy.
We took turns negating our worth,
from pheromone fixes to sex sickness.

We were puddles of electrified water,
waiting for the innocent in midnight basements.
We were brass knuckles
and the bottle of whiskey at all-ages shows.

We were church pew evil,
hoping to firestorm cleanse the world
of all impurities.
We were shaven heads and Mohawks
steel toed boots and violent empathy.
We were children fed Adam's apple
giving the finger to regret.

There is something glorious about feigned apathy,
by a flock of broken promises
and failed vows.

We never expected to live this long.

We cannot find enough apologies,
so we throw our bodies onto funeral pyres
hoping we can effigy ourselves absolved.

We are very, very sorry;
not for the stain we left,

but remaining waking pillars
of your failure.

All we ever wanted
were the lies we dressed ourselves in
to billboard us proud.

Poetry Sucks

Poetry is a kick in the nuts
still throbbing long after the tears dry
and the culprit has forgotten about said kick.

Poetry has hated me my whole life
whipping Kunta Kinte in the pit of my stomach
making fire from my eyes
to warm my fears.

Poetry has been running circles around me
since I first learned to write the difference
between you and me.

Poetry is the bane of my existence,
my life sentence; to never be
able to see the world as you do.

Fistprints

You speak of non-violence
yet your head cocks like a gun
shooting bullets, dressed as words.

I write poems with fistprints
reading skull fragments and splatters of blood

as if they were tea leaves
and palm lines.

tweeker

the tweeker danced around the pool table
attempting to look as suave as
crystal methamphetamine-induced psychosis
would allow.

from buttoning to unbuttoning
leather vest, covering and exposing
hairy chest, always leaving naked
the homemade Golgotha crucifix tattoo.

he danced the spun ducky woo woo dance
round and round, flailing arms and stick
above condensed poet brains
as we sat there

huddled to write
we discussed
Ginsberg and New Mexico,
soccer and line breaks,
and who was driving
between the two poetry
readings that night.

I realized then
that I was not a poet
but a single twitching
exposed nerve ending

in the sole body
that is language.

Maldito

my name is Johnny, and I am an alcoholic
my name is violence, and I am a scared little boy
my name is hatred, I have lost my way

mi nombre es no bueno, estoy maldito
yo naci maldecido

we were cursed from underneath
bleacher conception
our only Irish luck is not having been aborted
though most of us
view this as a curse

we are not victims
but still feel justified
in our bitterness

we are scoundrels
and degenerates,
corrupted by decades of fear

we peacock feather, chest out
laugh at all things we cannot understand,
which are all things

we want nothing more than
to be a part of this alien world,
but find contentment
with tools of intimidation
to keep ourselves from
appearing vulnerable

we are not forgotten, but wish
we were, giving us the excuses
needed to perform such
vile summoning of inner demons
we are so accustomed to

it is a lust for death and
a fear of life, that keep us
barricaded in dreams of anarchist ideals

we bleed indifference
and exhale hatred,
but we are hopeless romantics as well

we understand the intimacy of color
and read Rimbaud through windshield tears
and latch on to every painful hope
that comes down the pike at us

we are still little boys
holding out for the divinity of the first kiss
and the home of lovemaking

do not fear me as I fear you
I am just a recently uncaged animal
bred in captivity, looking for a home
amongst you

I will share with you
my suffering
so that you know
no one walks alone

Barfly

I watched him as he stumbled out of the bar
wearing a broken heart
beautifully upon his sleeve

he slipped on a metal grate
wet with rain
and on the open sidewalk
he pounded his fists
and stomped his feet
as he screamed into the night sky

I heard clear *her* name

the harmonious cry erupted from his lips,
lips which just previously
slurred and gargled obscenities

but the *name*

the name was clear as church bells,
as if it were the password
into the gates of heaven

and in all this wet drunken commotion,
never stained,
stayed the still beating
broken heart
decorating his sleeve

Burnt-Bottom Spoons

We are laudanum-drenched sugar cubes,
dripping life over flaming sweetener
into the bitter green absinthe of youth.

We are bridles in the teeth
of fantasies of hope,
trying to rein in the depravity
that is the mediocre of us,

tainting the sour truth
with anything to take the edge off,
yet always overcome
by our own delusions.

We are bits of cotton
pulled from burnt-bottom spoons
hoping there are enough remnants
of yesterday's hope to sustain us
till we are capable of finding
something new and forever.

Pandora's Bottle
for my father

you held my hand in your stern
unforgiving
calloused embrace

as your seedling cried
bemoaning a mother's abandonment

you tried to mold me
into your image

frustrated by the lack of enthusiasm
you grew bold in a foreign land

desperate attempts to chisel
life blood integrity

to only conceal the disappointment
with barren drop of death

drowning in our shared bane
amber queen anne's lace

I see your pain
as you lost your balance

the fatherhood foothold faltered
falling down

just as I fall now

I know your pain now
and I forgive you

I only hope that you find me
worthy of your father's name

as I make my way in the world
that never understood you

Bleached Brown Leather White

When he saw his blood-caked socks
as he removed the dusty shoe, he realized
the road was longer than he hoped.

Leather toe casing ripped from the sole
exposed his aching feet to the rocks
and hardened, rabid earth.

He couldn't remember
the last time he saw shoelaces.

The sun had bleached the brown leather white
and the shape could no longer be recognized as shoe.

Sweat rolled off the tongue gangplank from his ankle.

Rubble and dust and blood gather around his feet,
like tumbleweeds.

Ode to Tom Waits

My heart always feels like closing time;
last call, no more booze, no one to ride the train with.

But you, you sing me all the way home,
and sometimes to sleep.

My dad first pointed you out in *Dracula*
and then played you on the ride home.

Later, you sang to me *Bottom of the World*
while I was in fact, at the bottom of the world.

We would *Big in Japan* the night away
at the Yamhill Pub.

And I always dreamed of an *Ol' '55*
even though I have never seen one.

I'm not really sure of what 55 you sang,
but I have one in my veins,
it drives all day
through the freeways of my body
stops for a drink at my heart
every day around 10pm
and stays there till closing time,

singing old Irish tunes and folk songs,
and praying I don't fall in love
with the girl who couldn't be bothered,
praying to a god we only see in the movies.

Caring and sad and unavailable,
going home alone and in love,
you are always singing

in a voice too cold to comfort me,
but too bold to live without.

Gin

they never heard the calling
angelic choir
screaming clang of emergency siren

they never saw the beauty of it
the Matisse watercolor
sun blazing through clouded cylinder

how could they understand that gin
tastes like children's laughter

that the absence of it is more overwhelming
than the consequences

empty glass panic
empty bottle broken heart

they don't understand
what would compel a man
to drink gin straight
at burning eyes, twitching skin daybreak

fearing the terror
that sniper waits
on the other side of morning

violent convulsions amongst
wispy mouse trail hallucinations
like the morning I woke up in the drunk tank
talking to a German Shepherd named Philippe

(Philippe wasn't there)

they don't understand
how women can trade dignity
for slurred speech utopia

or why the ones in trench coats
choose doorways over detox

gin

the glue
that held pall mall delusional world
together at busting seams

the kind word at just the
right moment of heart break

the breath of relief
at the sight of bomb shelter hatch
noticing approaching tornado

gin was the only thing that loved me
the way I wanted to be loved
brutally tender
and without prompting

gin was the poligrip that kept
my teeth from chattering

and when I put it down, I wondered
if I could ever sing the blues again

when I put it away

my head sagged, crooked door frame
and I questioned my purpose

I question my purpose now

you see,
the gin doesn't sing me to sleep anymore

and I don't get enough rest
and my bones are hollow
and my lungs taste icicles
and I can't find the knob
to turn down the volume
of my screaming heart
and I am afraid

what I haven't told you

every night
that I go home alone

every night
I think I can smell juniper

my two disasters
for John and Mimi

I wouldn't wish either of you on anybody.
I wouldn't wish anybody on either of you.

Take it for what it is.

Take these words as the wedding present
you didn't see coming.

Take each other and run.

Spend each other liberally,
like complimentary poker chips,
on secret weekend getaways.

Show the world that nothing can be more beautiful,
or frightening,
than two people who find purpose
in each other's eyes.

Yell.
Yell at each other,
and with each other,
as if the echo of your passion
gives the world direction.

Load whispers into each other
like bullets.

Push each other's buttons.
Light each other's fuses.

Remind us that we enjoy watching things burn;
not an Oakland Hills blaze, decimating all
audacious enough to breathe near it, but
a fucking big bang, breathing life into the
emptiness that surrounds
your perfect storm.

Give each other headaches
that only butterfly kisses
in candlelit bathtubs can heal.

Raise each other up
like you're raising the minds
and the hearts of the little ones around you.

Tear each other down
so that you both are still capable
of compassion in the vulnerable moments.

Don't worry about money,
not this time.

If you love
each other like you are supposed to,
the god you do, or do not, believe in
will see to it that you are taken care of.

Take care of each other
'cause I can't count on you
to take care of yourselves,
but GODDAMN you are magnificent
in your aptitude for caring.

And, when all else fails,

hold each other,
like Icarus held his dreams
of the sun.

Hold each other *at* people,
like a last belligerent *fuck you*
to the non-believers.

Like Bonnie and Clyde
were nothing more than a sideshow.

Like Thelma and Louise
were just tourists.

Fucking *hold* each other.

It's bumpy
and frightening as all fuck,
but I'd be lying
if I said you don't make
that shit look good.

When you hold each other,
pull your bodies apart
ever so slightly.

Look down.

Can you see that glow?

Can you hear that?

That is the rest of us
humming gospel sanctuaries

as close to your heart as possible,

trying to remind you
to hold each other,

'cause this
is precious.

facebook chain post

I was raised to fear silence,
to put my hands over my head to
protect it from direct blows,
to not complain,
and to get what's coming to me.

And that booze, drugs, and sex
are waaayy more important
than my parents' children.

I was taught to take from people
before they have a chance to take from you.

That fear is more functional
than respect.

And that the world
does not
give a
fuck
about you.

If you were raised this way,
fuck reposting.

Instead,
take your revenge.

Once Innocent

We were innocent once
before we grew afraid
and started to feign dignity.

We were children once
looking to get lost in the mystery
that tomorrow would leave on our doorsteps
every morning.

We sang,
never cared if we were in tune
or if we even knew all of the lyrics.

We danced before we learned to walk.

We spoke the language of God.

I mourn the tidal wave of experience
that every poet yearns for.

I forgot more than I ever fucking knew
in the first place.

Porn Store Two-Step

I get off the train and realize
it's right there on the corner.

I wrestle with my intentions
and my bank statement
and against my better judgment
and decide to check it out.

I open the door.

jingle jingle

The place smells of sweat and self-hatred.

Toys and gleeful gadgets line shelves
in crystal-enclosed cases.

The pairs event naked ballet
glares down at me from dusty monitor.

I turn right on the airport rug and
come face to shriveled face
with men conversing
way too naturally for such a place.

But, the dialogue is so refreshing.

It almost tectonically pushes
the regret high enough that,
if I get down on my knees,
I may be able to recover my dignity.

I brace myself against waves of
run! and I slowly move to
plastic rows of plastic cases.

The cases are empty.

Their contents are hidden in
earmarked drawers behind hand-greased counters,
but the cases illustrate invigorating images
that tell of the hours of turmoil ahead.

Droplets of self-pity rain from my brow
as I peruse the only sanctioned relief
for a man of my sort.

I'm not exactly sure what I am looking for,
but I am sure something will arouse my interest.

The big numbers in the corners
of these boxes
are a major player
in the decision-making process
for us frugal porn purveyors.

I want more bang for my buck.

I want to look into the eyes of the women
on the screen
and imagine that those eyes,
full of cocaine and stage lighting,
are just for me.

That they think of me
and get as lonely as I do.

I wonder if
porn stars write poems
about their failed aspirations
and ink out determination
in the same world
that seems out to get us all.

Sounds Like

What my parents sounded like
when they would talk in the kitchen,
I imagine, is a lot like
looking at someone I love
when they are unaware.

They sound like science fiction.
They sound like daydreams.

Much like those of an IBM,
carefully mapping out ways
to achieve the impossible,
but only ever coming up with radio static.

My mother left when I was three,
my father died when I was fourteen;
fear and nausea were the only home
I had ever known.

I have been trying to prove to the world
that I am a man of principle,
but I still remember the sound of my father
pinning my mother down,
tickling her till she peed herself,
then breaking her nose for peeing herself.

Maliciousness comforts me.

Like the sound of a toothbrush
being scraped across cement prison floors
comforts a convict.

We seek not moments without pain,
just something familiar.

I never liked heroin, but the familiarness
of junk sickness and hypodermic relief
was enough to keep me strung out
for thirteen long years.

When I find myself
crunching numbers of improbability,
trying to calculate myself back to innocent,
I get lost in the static.

Wind between Skyscrapers

I'm on the bus,
heading home from a panic attack,
running as fast as thirsty legs
will carry me,

yet, every time I roll west across the bridge
I see your face, no matter where I am,
how I feel, what I've done,
or who I'm with,

you're always smiling at me.

and I get brought back to me
where I can rest my head on dreams
and the hope of the man I am becoming
massages my tired eyes.

you are my Mona Lisa,
complete with mohawk and face tattoos,
but a purity that runs so deep
that if I gaze into your eyes long enough
I can remember how it felt
to be an innocent child

before we learned about self-doubt,
taxes, and unattainable beauty,

when everything was possible,
except tomorrow, 'cause right now
was still so wonderfully overwhelming

when hope didn't feel like carrying
dead friends on broken backs

when the breeze still tasted of tangerines
and girls still had cooties

when sex didn't equate worth, but our intimate
relationship with laughter did

I see your face, and I smile.

I trace the thought of your curves with bashful fingers
wondering what thoughts course through your head,

this feels like I'm undressing you.

I know I should probably tell you how I feel,
but I still get nervous when I look at you

'cause your radiance reminds me
how truly vulnerable I am.

the kind of fragile I try to hide from the world:
that I still love the movie *Some Kind of Wonderful*
and I still listen to Peter Cetera
when I think no one is watching

that it's not the macabre that I like about Poe,
but the magnitude of his capacity to love
that would twist a man so.

you remind me that dawn
is a choir of birds,
who sweetly gospel me awake

and that dusk is really
just a parade of mischief
as we pray we can play "make believe"
one last time, as we run around
on our first night of summer
at the end of our senior year.

trying to be adults,
but still too naïve for calloused hearts.

Portland,
on this night,
the first of our whole lives,
run with me as we laugh poetry
onto city streets where we cried.

let's see if we can forget what loneliness feels like
and remember the fear of dawn,
hoping this night will never end.

we can walk the train tracks back to a time
when we were alive, and the wind between skyscrapers
would kiss us lucky somehow,
always getting away from the cops.

we can wave at cars on the highway
boldly assuming they run away
like only lovers seem to be able to

Bonnie and Clyde fleeing to a hideaway
to hold each other through the night,
praying to never see the sun again

and we will hold each other's

free spray-paint-under-fingernailed hands
so tightly as if trying to show the world
that there is still room for hopeless romantics.

Portland,
thank you for taking me back,
after all I've put you through,
every unkind word from this fragile heart of mine,
you still forgave me.

So, for that, in thanks,
I will remember our nights together,
just me and you,

and how you loved me
till I was capable of loving myself.

How to Decimate Loneliness in Ten Easy Steps

1.
Stop reading this poem and look into the eyes of the one
to whom yours seem to belong to these days. They may
look back.

2.
The awkward feeling you are having right now is not
love, it is nausea, and you both have it. We all get it. So
stop listening to your diffidence and just say hello.

3.
You know what, stop listening to me. I have no idea
what I am talking about. I couldn't find my way out of a
self-loathing day spent alone playing *World of Warcraft*
wishing I had somebody to lightly brush my hand and
remind me that I am not alone.

4.
Who really is ever truly alone? It's not like I don't have
friends, I do. They just have more important people to
go home with and have coffee with and laugh with and
watch movies with and fight with and have sex with.

5.
Didn't I tell you to stop listening to me? My nights are
spent wet and cold in my pajamas, trying not to log
on to a multitude of personals sites to chase away the
hollow.

6.
What about suicide? People tell me that's selfish, but

Amy says it's selfish to not let me. And then I get stuck running circles in valleys of thought I am not supposed to be in.

7.
BOOZE!!! Booze can be the greatest friend you have ever had, so drink, in abundance, the strongest alcohol available. Do it publicly so, maybe, just maybe, you and that beautiful girl, who is just as drunk as you, might be magnetically pulled to each other and you can nakedly make believe the other person knows you well enough to love you, as you both just masturbate with each other's bodies.

8.
Since when did people start asking me for advice? Leave me alone.

9.
I don't ever have to have that which I love, and have come to depend on, taken from me.

10.
There is nothing lonelier than being left standing in the cold of an empty bus stop watching the bus take the person you thought would finally validate you away.

You're soaked to the bone, and without enough money to drink away the rising tide of alone.

for the one-armed junkies

the Houdini to my intravenous Evel Knievel
how gracefully he holds spoon between toes

the ferocity with which he plunges
the steel into sutured stump

teeth gripping tourniquet
he dances the nod bop jazz dance

always looking for phantom veins
in phantom limbs, always calling Seymour

and talking to decomposing rooftop friends

Real Muthaphuckkin' G's

I want to do for literature
what Eazy-E did for hip hop,

keep it gangsta.

talent torn from concrete streets,
shaking hands, selling souls,
art dripping blood from slit throats.

I want my poetry to be banned and picketed,
rejected as violent
and lascivious obscenity.

as voluminous rhetoric fades
my neon genius
hums.

intrigue can kiss my ass

we spend our whole lives
watching sappy movies, reading romance novels
till we're running around like sheep
trying to buy into lonely fantasies
expecting people to read our minds
putting desires and needs on back burners
chasing illusory ghosts
of unspoken electric spark connections
and happy endings.

Patron Saint

In 270 A.D., Claudius II, Emperor of Rome, outlawed marriage. He believed that married men made bad soldiers since they were reluctant to be torn from their families in the case of war.

Claudius also outlawed Christianity. There could be no other god above the supreme god, the Emperor of Rome.

Valentine was the bishop of Interamna. He saw the Emperor as oppression deified, believed people should be free to love and love God. So, Valentine invited young couples to him and united them in secrecy.

Claudius eventually discovered Valentine's mutiny, but, favoring his conviction, he offered Valentine a chance to redeem himself; leave the cloth of Christ, and join Rome in service of the Roman God.

When Valentine refused to renounce the Son of Man, an enraged Claudius sentenced this "enemy of the state" to a three-part execution.

While in prison, awaiting his demise, Valentine fell in love with the jailer Asterius' blind daughter. Because God so favored Valentine in his devotion to God and to love, God granted the boon of sight to the captor of the heart that had sought to free the hearts of others.

The day the once blind daughter of Asterius opened her new sight-filled eyes, Valentine earned the title "Saint."

On February 14th, 270 A.D., Saint Valentine was first beaten, then stoned, and finally decapitated.

A note was found in his prison cell to his beloved signed, "From Your Valentine."

We are precision-guided missiles sent to decimate all that stands in the way of the true supreme god, Love.

Saint Valentine knew of our capacity to sacrifice all that is dear to us, in the service to the one true deity. He saw no difference between love, war, and the vulnerable hearts of humans.

We have been loving disasters, causing glorious destruction of ourselves, and leaving nothing but solidarity and love poems in our wake.

I question the difference between "lover" and "warrior."

Ask any soldier, ask any poet, what compelled them to commit such courageous acts of atrocity throughout the centuries and they will strike up in harmonious accord, "LOVE!"

Do not be fooled by Hallmark. Instead, listen to the ghost of Saint Valentine.

This love business is a dangerous game.

night crawler limbo party

Dreams are city buses,
always on time, and my
watch has been slow,
since I can remember.

I wear disheartened
like an old baseball cap,
dirty with sweat stains,
with memories of Wade Boggs,
cleanliness is overrated.

Lack of opportunity
screams from beneath my shirt
like Tom Jones' chest hair.

I have been domesticated
and fluent in failure
for quite some time.

How do you say "mediocre" in ....

I strove for under-achievement.

I thought if I wasn't going to be good at anything,
I would be really good at not being
good at anything.

Although, I wasn't exactly a slacker.

I worked very hard
at making sure the standard was so low

that night crawlers would have to crouch down
to get beneath the bar I set.

Standards were only for those
who could afford them.

Luckily, I have always been poor
so I can't afford to be bothered
with such things as dignity.

I still remember

I still remember how you feel

how your butt rested perfectly
on my cupped hands

how I couldn't take my eyes
off of you, when you wore
that tank top, the one cut
so the bottoms of your breasts
hung avocado perfection
beneath

how we could lay there for hours
failed attempt after failed attempt
to count each strand of
radiant sunset hair

how each outfit, no matter
how shabby, would jump with
joy, and shine electric sparks
just from touching you

I still remember how you could
throw everything away
just to agree with my bad ideas
because you knew that is how
I like to make love

I still remember how you dove into
my world, head first
and how quickly I fell in love

with the fact that
you hate safety nets

I even remember
how your cutesy laugh
accepted my drug- and self-pity-
induced infatuation
with early nu-metal
and how you adopted it as
your own

But, I also can't forget
the tears, pleas, begging cries,
asking me to stop

stop using, stop crying,
stop punching, kicking, screaming,
stop running, fighting, lying,

stop leaving …
stop leaving you …
stop leaving you alone ….

Rah-Rah Words

You may think I write only rah-rah words,
but they translate into love poems
through a lens of decades of dried tears
I wear broken like a neon crown of thorns,
distilled through fits of fist speech.

But, I stopped looking for a new England
long ago.

So, I pickle my bones in absolutes, disdain,
and soapboxes.

I am no Viking warrior.

You will not see me in Valhalla when you get there
but rather haunting the landscapes of men
I wish I could have been more like.

Men I wish I laughed like;
smiled like.

On my best days, I feel as if I can't
notes from underground scoff correctly.
I can't even cower like real men do.

With wide open skeleton closets,
I will try to awkward my way into your heart,
wear my failures like a bright purple bow tie,
never going unnoticed.

Hoping, against all odds,

that my confidence does not shine through
because it gets misunderstood as swagger.

Hoping to reclaim innocence
and remember the holy
of our First Kiss.

Shod Foot

By noon, it had already been a long day.

Released from Cambridge City Jail
just the night before, I found
my way to the weeds beside
the Harvard Boathouse, the place
I was calling home those days.

Unable to fall asleep,
worrying about the outcome
of the assault and battery
with a deadly weapon charge
I was facing thanks to my antics
which got me locked up in the first place,

I dragged myself from the river bed,
hazy-eyed and thirsty, to see if
I could find a drop or two
of what my body was calling for.

When I got into Harvard Square,
Captain Jack, the old homeless
Listerine-drinking wino, had
somehow found himself a handle
of Jim Beam. So, I got Dr. Pepper
with my food stamp card, and we started
the day off right.

5:30, in the purple dawn of day,
I was already well on my way
to the kind of drunk I needed to

be to keep myself from thinking
about how her red hair,
mixed with my overdose blue,
would match the color of the sky
famously.

By 7:00, we were already screaming
out-of-key Muddy Waters tunes
at Ivy League passersby.

By 9:00, I was coming out of a blackout
lighting a crack pipe, sitting in the middle
of the JFK Harvard School of Law's
grassy knoll.

Yup, I was drunk.

By 9:30, Chunks and Mutt
were on their way down to the river
to drink and invited me to come along.

I don't know where I got the boots,
nor the identical serving of the
morning's shared breakfast,
but when I woke up in Harvard Square
with my own half gallon of Old Jim,
it really wasn't surprising.

When the weekend warrior orphans who
scurried around the Pit woke me up asking
me to fight their battles for them,
this wasn't really new either.

I was known as one

who would drink for the sake
of the horror stories I could tell,
and I would fight for the sake of
inflicting the same pain as I felt.

They pointed,
I staggered and swung,
never missing my mark,
my target went down.

I instantly sobered up,
kicked once in the face,
then reached down,
grabbed the blur I had forgotten
was a fellow human,
and tossed him down the escalator.

When we got to the bottom,
me and his lifeless body,
I dragged his head to the corner
between concrete floor
and concrete wall
and proceeded to kick newly-found
steel toes into his face.

I didn't know this man,
and I didn't care.

my mother abandoning me
with a violent drunken father
to cook meth in the woods
    (KICK)

my father marrying

wicked-whiskey-voice stepmother
who only wanted money and status
    (KICK)

who treated me like Cinderella
mocking me while I did
the chores he would beat her
for not getting done
    (KICK)

when evil stepmother left,
I became my father's
ten-year-old sparring partner
    (KICK)

getting bullied into breaking
into school to steal lunch money
and getting sentenced
to five years at Oregon Youth Authority
    (KICK)

father being murdered
    (KICK)

becoming a homeless orphan
    (KICK)

getting strung out on heroin
    (KICK)

getting married
and being unable
to even be a husband
    (KICK)

chasing wife 3,000 miles
to be asked for a divorce
   (KICK)

AND NOW, I CAN'T STOP
FUCKING DRINKING!!!
   (KICK)
   (KICK)
   (KICK)

The paper called the beating
of the India-born Harvard professor
racially motivated,
that the culprit was obviously
a white supremacist
due to the fact of his haircut
and footwear.

I had become the bigot
I had always fought
with the utmost prejudice.

Whatever my intentions were was overshadowed
by the violent drunken menace I had become.

While trying me for my second
assault and battery with a deadly weapon charge
in under 48 hours,
causing forty thousand dollars
of emergency reconstructive surgery
as well as trying to stop the internal bleeding
and release some of the pressure in
Mr. Adib's hemorrhaging brain,

the judge called it "Shod Foot."

I call it being a terrified little boy
trapped inside a man's body.

Besides,
it had been a really long day.

just another cold winter day

wake up to alarm soul
peanut butter and jelly
gray room has yet to feel home
cold feet
Boston punk rock on YouTube
bundle up, step out
public transit
coffee shop
stare at computer
write poem
delete written poem
smoke
asinine websites
smoke
write poem
delete written poem
smoke
wish for someone to talk to
not that person, dammit
look at exes' Facebook pages
write this poem
bundle up, step out
This is England '86 YouTube
smoke
internet porn
masturbate
try to sleep
smoke
punk rock YouTube
smoke
light off, eyes closed

cry
masturbate
lie awake
fall asleep at dawn
(maybe)
repeat repeat repeat repeat repeat repeat repeat repeat
repeat repeat repeat repeat repeat repeat repeat repeat
repeat repeat repeat repeat repeat repeat repeat repeat
repeat repeat repeat repeat repeat repeat repeat repeat
repeat repeat repeat repeat repeat repeat repeat repeat
repeat repeat repeat repeat repeat repeat repeat repeat
repeat repeat repeat repeat repeat repeat repeat repeat
repeat repeat repeat repeat repeat repeat repeat repeat
repeat repeat repeat repeat repeat repeat repeat repeat
repeat repeat repeat repeat repeat repeat repeat repeat
repeat repeat repeat repeat repeat repeat repeat repeat
repeat repeat repeat repeat repeat repeat repeat repeat
repeat repeat repeat repeat repeat repeat repeat repeat
repeat repeat repeat repeat repeat repeat repeat repeat
repeat repeat repeat repeat repeat repeat repeat repeat
repeat repeat repeat repeat repeat repeat repeat repeat
repeat repeat repeat repeat repeat repeat repeat repeat
repeat repeat repeat repeat repeat repeat repeat repeat
repeat repeat repeat repeat repeat repeat repeat repeat
repeat repeat repeat repeat repeat repeat repeat repeat
repeat repeat repeat repeat repeat repeat repeat repeat
repeat repeat repeat repeat repeat repeat repeat repeat
repeat repeat repeat repeat repeat repeat repeat repeat
repeat repeat repeat repeat repeat repeat repeat repeat
repeat repeat repeat repeat repeat repeat repeat repeat
repeat repeat repeat repeat repeat repeat repeat repeat
repeat repeat repeat repeat repeat repeat repeat repeat
repeat repeat repeat repeat repeat repeat repeat repeat

yup, I said it

I have never met a wise poet

'cause, if we were wise,
we would stop writing and
get on with our lives

Courtship

I sat there like a coward
hands wringing waterfalls of doubt
trying to read hidden intentions
into blatant come-on lines

she told me she "really" liked me
already explained how thick necks are a turn-on
while squeezing mine with
shivers for answers

but I wanted to play innocent

honestly, I always want to wait
for taxi cab horn blows
coupled with vibrant green lights
that would make the blind squint

I have always been afraid of those words
caressing my soon-to-be-broken ego
with *you're awesomes* and *I love you buts*

I am always hiding from the eventual
you're more like a brother landslides
or *I don't see you like that* nuclear wars

oh,
and it sure didn't help
when she explained how the
guy lost points
on their second date
today

when he tried to open the door

chivalry, a day too late

my head hung like war-torn flag tatters
and any courage I had gathered
were drowned under the melting ice cubes
I was now swirling in my watered-down Coke

she asked me, "What's wrong?"

I could vomit in the gravel
being kicked around by my feet

so, I told her the truth

I told her I was going to ask her out,
but now that I found out she was
already dating someone,
I didn't want to overstep my boundaries

you see,
while my peers were going to high school
testing limits, experimenting with the opposite sex,
learning to drive, getting their first jobs,
taking girls to drive-ins, dreaming of baseball,

I was sitting in a jail cell,
testing limits, experimenting with poetry,
reading *On the Road*,
cutting prison bars with Eldridge Cleaver,
learning that cinema is the villain

while my generation

was learning algebra,
studying the Spanish Inquisition,

I was learning the cartography of veins
and how to cook meth without blowing anyone up
and the perfect chemistry
of how many parts cocaine
wouldn't outweigh the effects
of how many parts heroin

so, regardless of many villainous attributes
I have cultivated throughout the decades,
there is an innocence

never been on a date
never made the first move
just recently learned how to be afraid

she saw that and said,
"I'm not doing any serious dating at the moment,
so, I am not adverse to that."

I greedily bit the bait,
"So, can we go out sometime?"

at the age of 31,
this is the first time
I have ever asked a girl out

Stand Your Ground

I can't tell you how many times
I've thought about making the
big jump;

climbing 37 flights of stairs
to inch tiptoe over the lip of the roof,
bringing knees to chest,
dropping the body,
raising the heels,
tilting forward at exactly
sixty-two and a half degrees,
pushing with all of my might,
as if standing to attention
out of a dead sleep.

To feel momentary weightlessness
until gravity meets rush of wind
against my stubble cheeks,
against my burning eyes,
against my contorted mouth
stuck somewhere between horror
and relief.

This is the only moment
I will ever believe in destiny.

But, what if?

What if the Earth's rotation and the stratosphere,
couldn't catch up to me fast enough,

and I just floated away?

And, having broken such unalterable
laws of the universe,

I would float fluidly through constellations
and asteroid belts.

I would dance with sun flares
and chase comets.

I would ride shooting stars around Saturn's rings
and whisper sweet nothings into Pluto's ears.
(She's been so depressed lately,
since the universe disowned her.)

But then, the novelty wears off,
as it does with every relationship.

Because, people can't breathe in space,
and there is no one there to talk to,
and I realize that I'm lonelier now
than I have ever been in my whole life,
and I wish I had never jumped.

Stand your ground.

Stand your ground,
I promise, it gets better.

Stand your ground for everyone
that knows lonely squeeze-pillow sobs
note for note.

Stand your ground
for the playground fat kids.

Stand your ground
for the tick-tock clock watching tweekers
dreading library closing time.

Stand your ground
for the nameless panhandlers
you could not ignore on your way home tonight.

Stand your ground
for Mormon missionaries,
Jehovah's Witnesses,
Hare Krishnas,
and telemarketers,
someone's got to love them.

Stand your ground for teenage mothers.

Fuck that.

Stand your ground for teenagers,
that shit's hard.

Whatever your reasons,
stand your ground. Plant your feet.

'Cause it's fucking cold up there.

Brass Balls

You want soul?

Well, I've got a pair of brass balls.

I didn't write this for
the Amiri Barakas
or the d. a. levys
or the Sapphires,

but for us.

We misshapen mutants
made from mistakes of
essence-nurturing generations before us

we punks, we skins,
we crack pipe metalhead seraphim.

We are souls left behind
by Duke Ellington
dandled upon Burroughs pedophilic knee
forced through a rusting sax
by the nouveau hippie beatniks.

Forced to dumpster-dive,
wipe off the mold and maggots,
and feast with such desperation
that one may think us famished.

Hungry?
Yeah.

But not in the literal sense.

Not like a need to fill the belly
or wash away the taste of hipster semen,
but hungry for the blood of those
who left us to rot.

Depraved animals we be,
smiling at the thought of
gnawing on the bones of our heroes
pissing upon their graves
marking our territory
like feral cats
stomping through their ghettos
with such bravado
it would make mighty Rome tremble
at its knees.

America,
we write the disenfranchisement
and disdain you have given birth to.

And yet, we point no fingers.

Fuck,
we practically idolize
you idolatrous imbeciles.

I just hope I don't end up
like Anne Waldman,

shouting another boring rendition of "Howl"
to a group of upper echelon Buddhist social activists.

The kind of people
who vilify the necessary violence
only the poor could know.

Who, having paid
a hefty six hundred dollars,
just sit and meditate
in a run-down barn
in rural Massachusetts.

Still shouting lines from "Howl."

Still shouting
as if it still means something.

a river runs through us

Your nephew found the last picture
we have of you, your grizzled face
stern behind the beard I wish I could
grow, in hopes of emulating you.

Your clothes, so simple, as if tattooed
beneath the blue plaid linen shirt is, "I am to
be counted as one among all men."

Never loosening the chain of men before
me, bringing up boys to become
oaks, stoic in their regard for a world
always appearing so alien, that the
only reprieve from our own fears

(fears packed away like photos of past lovers
only to be brought out when no one is looking)

was to escape to the roar of the river,
to learn the ancient dance of our tribe,
the art of casting a fly fishing rod.

With a pull, swing back, snap of the wrist,
you and Grandpa Ike taught me to make steel
hooks and string sing like a swarm and
soar like the most beautiful of birds.

Grandpa went upstream to his fishing spot
and I was sent downstream, yet both of you
were so close I felt choked.

In unison, we would *1 2 3 kiss* our questions upstream,
letting the wisdom of silent men flow down
to the next one.

I am still waiting downstream.
Still seven years old.
Still waiting to hear your reply.

Machine in the Middle

embrace the loneliness,
'cause eventually
it will be all we have left
to hold.

leave the sex and the sweat
to those with nothing better
to do.

leave the booze and the bullshit
for those who have never
tasted sanctity.

we have been compasses,
searching in dizzying circles
for direction.

talking to those yet to come
but they aren't here yet

and those who were here
but they are gone.

forever losing mechanics that
makes the whole thing work.

the machine in the middle.

Three parts truth

I was on break from the trend
factory floor when the news came
over the intercom that one of
our co-workers had been hit by a bus,
pulled under it, and dragged for three
Boston city blocks.

The news said that there was a trail
of smeared blood and limbs
as if they were articles of last week's
unwashed laundry on my
Dorchester apartment floor.

It was the middle of summer,
and the stench of decay and
the morose purple cloud of sorrow
that hung over Central Square
like a suspended sentence
kept people from hanging out
in Cambridge that night.

You could catch a couple of
curious collegiate eyes searching
the landscape for hidden remnants
of the man's body.

My friend Joe is the one
who was standing with him at
the bus stop.

My friend Joe is the one

who watched the terrifying scene
in slow motion.

My friend Joe is the one
who stopped traffic and finally
stopped the bus.

As tragic as this all is,
it is not uncommon,
until you meet the
uncommon man
who witnessed it.

Joe was always one
of our toughest.

He was always
the one you called when you wanted
someone to have your back.

He was the last person
you wanted angry.

He ate steak without
cooking it, or even killing
the cow first.

He ate people,
while waiting for
Matlock reruns.

He was sledgehammer-fist-mallets
and mortar-brick-thick skulled.

It is rumored that he even
tore someone's jaw completely off
before realizing he had the wrong guy
without so much as even a mea culpa.

So when I found him at his computer
that night, starting to play *World of Warcraft*,
twitching, the big brother Good Samaritan in me
had to ask what was up.

When he turned around, I heard
the sound of snot mixed with flapping wings
and saw his reddened tear-stained cheeks.

I didn't even think he was born with tear ducts.

I never expected to put my arms around him,
let alone have such an act so well-received.

Then and there, the scariest most violent person I know
sobbed and squeezed, and sobbed and squeezed.

I never understood how easily a heart can break
till I held Joe.

And when they talk shit about him
playing *World of Warcraft*, I keep secret
that, he is not playing, but hiding
from the eyes at the back of the bus
that took more than a backseat.

Dorchester

Dorchester, my heart,
your stinging snowflake kissed me
many January mornings
as I cried my way to work

I stood pinnacles atop Mount Ida Road
and watched storms protect Boston Bay
while dreaming of settlers facing
such harsh elements

how different are we from them
traveling vast formidable distances
to find shelter in landlocked bay arms

Dorchester, multifarious haven
for liberal-minded hoarders of culture,
even on all-American Adams Corner,
one can order coffee in Gaelic

and down the street, on Bowdoin,
one can taste jerk chicken
requested in Patois

there is no distance between
Cape Verdean, Jamaican, Irish,
artists, writer, and gay entrepreneur

yet one could call for help
and not be heard for years

your bleeding ears hear no calm,

but your caress knows no stranger

Dorchester, you gave me a home
when none could be found,
you gave me a friend
when I spoke a dead language

but even in Aramaic,
your borders understand the cries
of all misplaced working men

asylum of nefarious
redemption song singers

your butternut squash sunsets
greeting me as I rise from under
Old Harbor Projects

red steam rising to meet
your wave-crested kisses

but, when I looked down the line
of hard knuckled, dried tender men
crusted with oil, drywall, silica, fiberglass
and the glory of holding your family safe
in tear-stained working hands

Dorchester, Catholic cathedral freckled flatland,

I stopped being bothered
by your assumptive pontification of piousness
and just fell in love
with the city that gave birth
to the first housing projects in New England

'cause you wanted
to give every
wayward child
a home.

Her Cowardice is Beautiful

My mother plays "make believe."

She pretends I am not my father's son
and she wasn't sprouted from gin and disregard.

She has taken to waving banners that seek to
choke her as if complicity will keep her safe from
phantom fists and loneliness.

Her cowardice is beautiful.

Over the years, she has become
shades of broken and surrender,
till sarcasm is left hanging in the air
like the pink elephant of the mother
she never wanted to be.

She was a flower child. She will
tell you all about it, while juxtaposing
NASCAR and the Pledge of Allegiance.

If she was ever honest, don't expect it
of her now.

I am glad we never really connected, there is
less shame watching her decay.

I can only ever be a spectator. That is all either
of my parents ever prepared me for.

So What Yourself
~or~
Ms. Yarn Face

I was reminded of alive
as I watched strands of her yarn
get flung about in the same breeze
that first brought GG Allin to my ears.

I get caught up in the tragedy of survival
and worry that the permanence of my hands
will make me unable to teach.

We have tread moats around ourselves,
pacing the long steps
from yesterday to tomorrow
without stopping in between.

I have forgotten what it means to stand for,
or with, but have rallied against
as if my judgment was proof enough
for the forgiveness I have yet
to grant myself.

Can we still become the hope we lack
when paychecks short of relief
knock heart murmurs upon our
frail doors? Doors we only put into place
to keep ourselves free from the fears
which have kept us inside.

I am dancing right now
in my basement apartment,

reeking of feet and old food,
remembering that comfort
is only available when I decide
to be comfortable.

Is this poem good?
Does it need to be?
Will this get published?
Maybe someday.

But only when its success
does not get in the way
of its creation.

I am sitting

I am sitting,
peering at the bricks I had walked
when I discovered crystal meth,

listening to men giving orders,

and I cry, thinking about
how far we have come.

From the bridge bottom rooftop,
fire spinning, vapor coughing,
annihilation of chastity;

to the gut knotted, call back
phone calming, nod off
jingle jangle dance;

cooking breakfast
in burnt-bottom spoons.

And the billowing cloud of doorbells,
pulse knob turning, and the
endless scrape push, Brillo bounce
to get that one last hit
always sending me into a frenzy for more.

I walk these glimmering streets,
reflected in the tears of years of forgetting.

Forgetting the city's children
left to fend for themselves.

The hearts of these children,
already broken, but carefully
re-wrapped and pieced together,
litter street corners, shelter cots
and nightmares.

Even though their hearts won't beat on command,
they will remember when compassion first touched
their faces, when precious time was devoted
to acknowledging their existence,
whether they believe it or not

they will do great things.

Sometimes I sit on the corner of my youth,
watching with frenzied disdain.

Holding back fits of violent imagery
of brutally teaching them
street culture pecking order.

But, in times of reflection, I see
nothing more than children, bereft
of culture and parental concern.

Our world is more interested in blaming
our youth, criminalizing them,
telling them they are chemically separate
from their peers, medicating them
into a state of domesticated complicity.

In this moment, I release my jaw,
stopping the creation of grinding tooth dust,
and remember, above all else,

us.

And pray to always remember
what it feels like to be forgotten.

Make Believe

I have always wanted to be optimistic.
I find it endearing.

So, right now,
we are going to make believe.

We are going to make believe
that I haven't been trained to hate upon impact.

And when my eyes go wide,
it means I am looking for an opportunity
to invite everyone into my heart
for tea, free tattoos, and campfires.

We are going to make believe
that every time I get hit with flying rocks
it only makes me want to get bigger
so I can stand in front of you,
so you can hear the beauty of flight,
without feeling the stinging of stones.

I want to make believe
that my pen runs out of ink
every time I try to write anger.

Let's make believe
that we all know faith is a blessing
instead of the curse we have come to see it as.

That Jesus
wanted to unite all humans

against the sadness in our hearts
that creates greed and delusion
and makes competitors of us all.

Let's imagine,
in a world of philosophers
and three-legged dogs,
that the boring and mundane
holds just as much beauty
as the obscene and profound.

And that there are actually people out there
that don't see any race other than human.

And that I don't spit when I talk.

And we can talk each other out of
having a bad day.

Let us dream
new hairstyles and no taxes;
where pomegranates are in season
for so long that we stop calling them
"in season" but instead call them "in year,"
as if there was never a time when the
pomegranates weren't ripe.

A time and place
where we let our poetry and paintings,
our choir voices,
and the fact that everyone stubs their toe
be our teachers and teach us to make faith.

To make believe.

To make believers out of us all.

So we can carry our dreams around
in shiny red wagons.

And we can only toss our tears out by the thimbleful.
And even those tears are made from laughter.

Can you help make me believe? Please?

I think optimism would look
really good on me.

Where did I put my drink?

I want to get into trouble
mischief, fight, fuck

no baseball bats to parking meters
I mean to maim, disfigure, bleed

these quiet days, subliminal boredom
reading, writing, arithmetic
trying to outdo myself

when all I want
is to do someone
do someone in

juggling machismo and intellect
sobriety and chaos

I want to taste fire
and enjoy the burn

I want to remember the sound
of my heart breaking

I want to hear the sound
of bones breaking

I want to kick up dust
and not run for cover

I want the police to know me by name

I want riot squad intensity
Pavlov knee jerk reaction
cringe at the sight of me

I want to war paint my face
with boiling sweat of sex and caked blood

and sledgehammer
structures of infidelity
and statues of iniquity

I want next month to see me coming, run, and hide,
weeping the oncoming tide of retribution

I want to liberate people

let's liberate each other
free each other from the constraints
of clothing and insecurity

let us rip each other to pieces
with savage beauty

I want poetry orgies
with city streets littered with bodies
sweat, cum, blood, and frenzied skin

I want to surf the middle of the ocean
wearing underwear on my head
screaming like a chimpanzee on ecstasy

I want to do cartwheels on treetops
while seeing what fallen angels we can summon
if we sing the National Anthem backwards

I want to riot
naked

let's burn the four letter word hope
and build right now in its ashes

I want tomorrow and yesterday
to fuckin' die already
we have let them haunt us for too long

so let's fucking riot

Visionaries

The visionaries I know
hide behind curtains of disdain
with voices like lemons
that Shirley Temple herself
couldn't sweeten the delivery.

Visionaries don't run arms wide
into hailstorms trying to hug the world
or have orgies in the middle of the street
hoping the world will
actually give a shit.

Visionaries find themselves in back alleys
smashing whiskey bottles
over each other's heads
so they can get at
the last drop of relief.

Visionaries don't hitchhike into sunsets
wondering what's on the other side of the horizon
hoping to spread love
to the atrophied limbs
of the human condition.

Visionaries hop freight trains
trying to escape
the building tsunami
of regret and shattered pieces
of a botched existence.

Visionaries don't dream in colors

or speak in exotic tongues
for the masses
to find life's
meaning.

Visionaries scream in blacks and blood reds
while praying for death
or at least to survive long enough
to be able to forgive themselves
for having survived at all.

Backwards From Infinity

I fall in love
every day with young
hopeful beauty.

I fall in love with people
and the people
they will or will not become.

Men and women who trade away
the last vestiges of youth,
innocence, and idealism,
for fleeting moments
of connection to anything.

To bind themselves
to the bodies,
minds, and souls
of strangers.

To therefore become infinite
in the passing of traded passions.

To never be forgotten.

My heart goes out to them
on empathy-scribbled
paper airplanes
thrown from dark corner bars,
while counting backwards
from infinity.

I fall in love
with broken men
and broken women
who find themselves
seeking danger
at dead-end truck stops
in the ceaseless
quest for the eternal.

And this is the purpose of the poet:
to live a poet's life
dying every day
of a perpetually breaking heart.

Like a dayfly

Shit we do when
feeling lonely on a cold night
like watching random crap
on the internet

I found myself watching
videos of redemption
hoping to find the
Vietnamese Susan Boyle
on "Asian Idol"
or whatever the fuck it's called

So when the Korean boy
took the stage,
I noticed he was trying
to wring the stains of abandonment
from his hands

he said he was a dayfly

a bug

that travels aimlessly
from city street
to city street
from dumpster to
alleyway
without any one person
aware of his existence

he said he had been forgotten

like the love letter
from a secret admirer
that got lost
in the Sunday coupons
and thrown out
with the rest of the trash

he is the moment of honesty
that redeems us all

the tear that tells us
we are human

the crowd laughed at mangy hair
and boring outdated attire
not knowing he would change the world
he started to sing

and when he sang

it was like waves of the ocean
crashing into the ears
of a girl from Kansas
who wanted to see the Pacific
before she killed herself
because her parents
removed her name
from their chests
for kissing a girl

and when he sang

it was a gospel choir
filling the southern air

of Baton Rouge
after medical miracles
allowed a deaf man
of 42 years
hear for the first time

and when he sang

it screamed
like the signature
of black-eyed housewife
on a restraining order
finally free

and when he sang

I finally felt the envelope of home
feeling warmth for the first time
I knew everything would be okay

I too was a dayfly, lost in a sea
of harmonious self-doubt
wondering if I could ever wash
away things I will never know

wandering from city street
to city street, from dumpster
to jail cell, from lost cause
to generic Walmart-bought identity

and when he sang

so did I.

Her Name is Dissent

"We waited together for the cowards to come
Outgunned and outnumbered but we wouldn't run
No mercy, no quarter, they'll pay for their sins
Now lower the cannons the battle begins."
　　　　　　　– Dropkick Murphys – "Hang 'Em High"

She is a time bomb
strapped to the chest
of Portland
banging her heartbeat drum
to rally her brothers and sisters
and drink retribution.

Her name is Dissent
and she has come for
the blood oath promised her.

She has come for her mule and 40 acres.

She is the voice of forgotten millions
rising harmoniously
like a firestorm
burning all who reach for her,
yet cleansing the earth
to make way for new life.

She is shit-upon human rights.

She is the backbone of women
deemed illegal for trying to survive.

She is the junkie left out in the cold
by parents who couldn't bother.

She is freedom.

She is the ghost of Che Guevara.

She is the single bullet
saved by Zapatista, PLO, and IRA soldiers.

She will not be taken alive.

She is Bobby Sands' ignored meal.

She is the introspective sand
beneath Malcolm's feet
as he made his way towards Mecca.

She is the prison bars surrounding
Nelson Mandela, only making him stronger.

She is the clicking keys of
Mumia Abu-Jamal's typewriter
singing Philadelphia to sleep
so they can forget the world
persecutes those who care.

She is your breath of relief, stolen
coming to take it back.

She is your daydream,
told dreaming is for children,
now get back to work.

She is this poem.

She is the blood pumping
blue within our veins.

Will you rise with her?

Will you rise?

a fairy tale

Our last Christmas together,
while we lived under Ross Island Bridge,
you confessed you were a dream.

It was only a dream.

I had always wondered that myself.

It was surreal, our first night together
under the eucalyptus leaves
after watching you for weeks
panhandling across from
Fuck You Frank's Liquor Store.

Your red hair, with a single dread
would snicker at the wind
dancing up Haight from Market.

You were the most beautiful image I had ever beheld
as you spit smoke and sailor cursed
your way through your lunch break.

I pitied your close attention to fashion
but was thrilled when you would wear
that canary yellow and fish scale blue sundress
coupled with 14-eye steel toed Doc Martens.

You were the feigned innocence
I had been looking for my whole life.

You asked me for a cigarette,

I asked you for floor space.

I didn't expect that line to work.

You took me home, fed me
spaghetti, speedballs, and flesh.

We stayed up quoting Burroughs and Jourgensen.

I told you I like art-school dropout girls, you told
me you like Napoleon-complex street-punk boys.

It was dreamlike when you took me up
on my offer for inheritance refuge,
Portland methamphetamine
and impossible love.

It was like the movies
how my angry Sid Vicious
fell for your Nancy Spungen
promises of eternal partnership
with heroin kisses
that created the monster
you eventually had to save yourself from.

It seemed too good to be true
when you invited me to Boston.

But, like every hope carrot
dangled in front of my ass face,
I bit.

You confessed you were a dream.

Unfortunately, now,
I'm wide awake.

Dreaming out loud

you tell me we weren't born for this
that violence only begets violence

tell that to the wife
who has only ever felt relief,
outside of hijab,
after her bazooka-armed husband
has been laid to rest

tell Boston
that tea means nothing
and the queen was right the whole time

tell that to the death row inmate
counting days with prison bars
since he stopped the man
who raped his wife
from ever raping again

luxurious forest floors
decadent and virile in their destructive blossoming
could not make way for new life
without the erosion of old

I mean, what good was Martin Luther King Jr.?
Didn't his non-violence only lead him to get shot?

Do we forget the importance of martyrdom so easily?

I just want to help that process along

and fortify the affirmation
of standing one's ground
and dreaming out loud

hearts

I'm only going to tell you this once.

hearts don't belong on windowsills
like freshly baked cherry pies
warm, crumbly, smelling like summer
for nomadic on the lam villains
to steal away, like your breath on a cliff.

they should be thrown like boomerangs
at burning crosses
tearing down worlds built on lies
and come back
scarring us from our own passions
and rejection of ignorance.

hearts, built like machetes,
get wielded like Viking claymores
or get strapped to the chests of bank robbers
like pulled pin hand grenades
ready to blow apart
everything.

but we put them on paper
bleeding ink of vilified self
and shout them through moaning microphones
as if to justify our very existence
against lies we keep telling ourselves.

we are worth more
than mere words could ever recite.

for, instead of trying to
barricade our hearts closed,
we open our chests vulnerable,
showing the world yet again that
there is no such thing
as alone.

Kansas Pearl Diving

you tell me to be patient
that there is a nut for every bolt
that it only ever happens when
you least expect it

but I can't remember the last time
I had good morning kiss expectation
or slow dance neck nuzzle

just an ember, fighting for oxygen
on a blustery Seattle night
a craning of the neck
to hear soft touch ivory
electric blanket of fan brush snare

it's like being a pearl diver
in Kansas

you tell me to be patient
when patience is the same thing
that keeps me waiting for sleep

I have plenty of patience

I am just
very
very
tired

Shadowboxing Death

There is brutal beauty
in a heavy life worn fast

as if taking things for granted
was an art form.

Never expected to survive this long.
Never really wanted to.

I spent most of my earlier days
cheating life and shadowboxing death

grasping on to flesh pleasures
as if each moment is *it*.

As if this rush is the last one.
It doesn't leave a pretty corpse.

And getting there, these days,
is uglier than ever.

I used to tell myself that the next hit would either
kill me or it was going to be fuckin' amazing.

I chase my dreams now
like I used to chase the glass dick.

I'm either going to make it
or I'm going to die trying.

My mother, unfortunately,

is not so fortunate.

She sits in her room, dying from thirst,
waiting to die. She won't be waiting long.

She welcomes more darkness into her very face,
whose shining optimism once made me nauseous.

I ran, trying to escape fate, but the lonely heart of
an aging mother brought me back.

I don't know if I am supposed to be here.
To witness. To try to bring her back to life.

But I will not watch the grave come to meet her at her
bedside. I will not fall for the same thing she has.

I wasn't made from the clay of docility,
but of the storm of no tomorrow.

I guess she wishes for that.

For no tomorrow.

Alexander

Watching my nephew's first
water fountain experience,
the gleam in his eyes
as his first understanding of poetry
was the cool tingle
of water splashing between his toes.

This triggered the memory
of my first brush with awe,
as I realize that I may love
this child, more than I have loved
anyone or anything else.

His defiant charge,
the look of devious
in his smile, brings me
more joy than any romance
has ever provided.

I want to give him more than
I remember ever being offered,
like a principled man,
with whom he can cry,
then tell all his secrets.

So, Alexander,
these words
are for you.

Never listen to what your teachers tell you,
unless of course you agree,

'cause when you get older,
nothing will be more valuable
than your ability to think for yourself.

Find men on whom you can rely,
'cause without these men,
you might find yourself
perpetually lonely,
unable to find shelter,
in the bed of any woman.

Stand for something,
especially if you know you will lose,
'cause when people speak of you
they will speak of a man with passion.
Plus, everyone loves an underdog.

Eat only honesty.
Comfort tastes good,
but when you find yourself full
from feasting on sweet decadence,
you may accidentally ingest something
poisonous, in search of palate excitement.

Question absolutely everything,
especially yourself,
'cause when you find the answers
of your own shortcomings,
you will become that much closer
to those around you.

Give yourself elbow room
'cause you are just a fragile human being
with bad wiring, but when you

have room to breathe,
you will find the fortitude you need.

Forgive everyone.
The action may be unforgivable,
but the people should always be pardoned,
for they, like you,
are just fragile human beings
with bad wiring.

And, above all else,
the advice you give to others
should also be kept for yourself.

Just as I will keep this letter to you,
for me to always remember
these things I must never forget.

poetry is a dead church

poetry is a dead church
clawing at the back door
deformed, caked with dirt
and blood and depravity

poetry is a haunting melody
armed with a chainsaw (or is it a hatchet?)
keeping you on the edge of your seat
and your girlfriend clinging to your shoulder

poetry is crawling out of the television
seaweed hair covering intentions
coming for the retribution
it so rightfully deserves

poetry is standing outside your window
wearing one of many masks
hoping you come outside and play
where it will leave you

broken, cold, and alone

only to come back an hour later
without its mask
and showing its hideous face

reaching down,
not to pull you up,
but to hand you a pen and paper
telling you,

Life's hard,
buy a helmet,

and write your own fucking poem.

Acknowledgements

I would like to thank Tim Crowell and the Snipes, Lenny Lashley, Jon Cauztik, Leedz Edutainment and crew, Ken "Dining Establishment" Casey, Mike McColgan, Rick Barton, and Bryan McPherson for showing me the true definition of friendship and what is possible when you start dreaming out loud. If it wasn't for your friendship and inspiration, who knows where I would be; this book sure as hell wouldn't be possible.

I would like to thank Bucky Sinister, Eirean Bradley, Mike McGee, Tyler Atwood, John "Survivor" Blake, Leah Noble Davidson, Robyn Bateman, Amy Everhart, Aleks Stefenova, Josh Lubin, Davey Mac, Brit Shostak, Meg Waldron, Portland Poetry Slam, Sparrow Ghost Collective, everybody at Criminal Class Press, Hubris Press, and all the poets I met at the 2011 National Poetry Slam and who have featured in Portland. Your guidance and inspiration are absolutely necessary to my survival and evolution.

I want to thank University of Hell Press, Greg Gerding, Eve Connell, and Amy Chadwick for taking a chance on me. I know I am impossible at times and you never gave up on me. It is an honor to not be picked last for such an awesome team.

Again, extra special love to Bucky Sinister, Eirean Bradley, Mike McGee, and Brian Ellis for being my on call poetry advisory board. You guys gave me time, patience, and love when the rest of the world was too afraid to.

(Author Photograph by Jill Greenseth)

About the Author

Poet is not the first thing you would think of when looking at Johnny No Bueno. Johnny rose from the ashes of punk rock, alcoholism and heroin addiction, and homelessness to become a force to be reckoned with. Hailing from Portland, Oregon, he reached across the country by way of freight train and hitch hiking, making a home in Boston, where he got sober and reunited with his early childhood love: Poetry. Taking his inspiration from the San Francisco Spoken Word scene which produced the likes of David Lerner, Daphne Gottlieb, and Bucky Sinister, the Beat Generation, hardcore, and punk rock, Johnny fashioned his cold disdain and fiery passion with the words he had stolen from book and record stores nationwide. He has since returned to Portland to be a son to his aging mother, a college student, and the Web Administer at the Portland Poetry Slam. He also lords over poetry submissions as Poetry Editor at Criminal Class Press. He hopes one day to receive his MFA in Creative Writing and indoctrinate America's impressionable youth with ideas of anarchism and revolt through teaching poetry and literature.

UNIVERSITY OF HELL PRESS

CPSIA information can be obtained at www.ICGtesting.com
Printed in the USA
BVOW071639050513

319883BV00001B/3/P